FINDING POETRY, FINDING ME

FINDING POETRY, FINDING ME

Rebecca P. Bruckenstein

PURE INK PRESS

PURE INK PRESS

Paperback ISBN: 979-8-9875866-1-7
Ebook ISBN: 979-8-9875866-2-4

Library of Congress Control Number: 2023922016

Cover Design: Mad Studios
Illustrations: Olga Tropinina and various artists

English Translation of the Israeli national anthem, *Hatikvah*, in the poem,
Am Yisrael Chai, is from the Jewish Virtual Library website.

Published by Pure Ink Press
www.pureinkpress.com

To the strong women who helped define me:
Grandma Toby Cavan and Grandma Mabel Bruckenstein
Aunt Sandy Kramer and Auntie Dolores Janssen
Linsey Hickey and Wendy Weiss

And to all who have trod this path with me
and held me in their hearts, this one's for you.

CONTENTS

AUTHOR'S NOTE   1

FINDING POETRY   3

NOSTALGIA   13

SELF-DISCOVERY   51

COMMUNITY & ME   95

ACKNOWLEDGMENTS   133

"Whatever you choose to do, leave tracks. That means don't do it just for yourself. You will want to leave the world a little better for your having lived."

— RUTH BADER GINSBERG

AUTHOR'S NOTE

When I began this journey, I thought it would be easy to write. Initially, words poured from my fingertips—until they didn't. However, there were experiences I wanted to share and emotions I wanted to express and further investigate to discover myself and to discover our world. So I continued to push through the periods of writer's block. I continued to find myself searching for a creative outlet that felt right.

For the last few years, I had thought about writing many different genres of books: a memoir, a non-fiction book about international relations in the Middle East (this was the topic of my master's thesis), or a young adult historical fiction novel. These genres require a lot of dedication to plan, research, and lay out a practical outline and timeline, none of which felt conducive to the chaotic energy that seemed to be bubbling over.

I was on a search to find myself and to find a form of writing that could help me dig deep. Initially, poetry seemed like the option furthest away—until it wasn't. While I was on my self-discovery journey, poetry began to sneak up on me. I would see poetry in the people I met and hear it in my interactions with the world around me. Eventually, poetry infused itself into all five of my senses. When this began to occur frequently, I knew I landed right where I needed to be. I discovered I was finding new information and viewpoints through the lens of poetry.

Poetry demands so much of the individual who is writing and of the ones who are reading. Poetry connects to a place in our souls that remembers what our brains have perhaps forgotten. All at once, we are faced with this challenging dialogue inside of ourselves. One aspect of this journey that I feel has been particularly poignant is the search to find the right vocabulary to convey my emotions—a practice that has both inspired and tortured me.

Up until a few years ago, I didn't think I could write poetry. I knew I could write research and policy pieces, but I didn't think I was *deep* enough to write a creative piece that I could be proud of. During the beginning of the COVID pandemic, I began taking writing classes with a stellar group of people who have inspired and motivated me. As part of my profession, I also helped numerous authors publish their own books that tell a myriad of stories and share experiences from a global perspective. By helping others, I learned that while I may not know all the fancy terms, I do have what it takes to put together a poetry collection.

Through this collection, I hope to combine the personal and communal past, present, and future to showcase the trapeze-like nature of life. My personal journey has been filled with both sadness and joy. My story includes doses of hope and a sprinkle of magic. Poetry taught me that we can morph our past experiences, positive and negative, into a journey filled with knowledge and growth, and we can travel these new paths with more understanding, kindness, and empathy towards others. We can build communities that are more resilient and adaptable to our world's ever-changing environment. We need to combine our strengths and support those in need.

This journey will never be truly complete—we change our viewpoints every day as we adapt to our surroundings, discover our self-worth, and find success.

I continue to remind myself that we write poetry one word at a time, just like you live life one moment at a time. It is important to be present while staying aware of the past and balancing the pressure of the future. My therapist often mentions this quote: "We are not human doings; we are human beings." We must *be* as well as *do*. I hope this collection balances my experience of being and doing.

FINDING POETRY

Scribbles

I scribble words on pages for many purposes:
to discover connection and community,
to quell the voices in my brain that tell me I am alone.

While the scribbles take place in solitary moments—
on couches,
on trains,
in offices with closed doors—
I am not alone.

The world is so much bigger than just me,
than all of us.
I hope these words will connect with some,
bring us close enough
to bind our own pages.

Canvas

A page is like a blank canvas.
My words paint.
My keyboard is a paintbrush,
gliding across the page to
express my inner thoughts.
Share my creativity.
My canvas is empty
until it is streaked with lines
of the world
of my heart.

A Moment

I sit with myself in silence,
my thoughts circling,
trying to land upon this patch of grass.

I hate the silence,
the lack of motion.

I sit alone,
knowing that the external stillness
is no match for the cacophony within.

I pause a moment
and pick up my pen.

Awoken

In my dreams, I hear
words of poetry.

Sometimes awoken with a start
to create.
Sometimes lulled to sleep.

Often,
I wish I could remember the words
that come in this twilight state.
Only leaving a trail behind.

Treasure Trove

I pause
to think about
all the words that
go unwritten or unsaid
that never leave my fingertips
or are never fully formed on my lips
the words that are only fragments within my core
I must adventure within to unlock this hidden treasure trove

Creation

The urge to create,
to document,
to share,
to experiment,
pushed me here,
outside of the only box
my mind has ever known.

This overwhelming urge
fills every cell,
is there with me,
even in my darkest moments,
where inspiration lurks in the shadows.

Creation carries me near,
far,
and into your arms.

NOSTALGIA

Moments

A laugh.
A cry.
A moment in time.

We pause.
We only know our past;
the future is yet to be.

Emotions are present,
but we can only feel
these fleeting moments.

We stop to marvel at the moments
along the way that last for mere seconds,
yet we remember.

Theater Nerd

In high school, I wanted to be cast in anything the
school provided as extracurricular in the arts.
I needed to e x p a n d my creative energy
in

some

W A Y.

I showed up for every audition,
sang, danced, acted,
pushed myself to the brink of exhaustion.
I stressed about the cast list with my peers,
and when the list would be posted for all to see,
my name rarely made it.
I found myself in ensembles,
highlighted (or pitied)
for my kindness.

It hurt the most when I was never cast at all.

I found a family
under the stairs,
became a part of the crew
behind the curtain,
without whom
the stage would be barren,
only a ghost light shining.
Even then, I didn't grasp the importance
of the roles out of the spotlight.

I didn't grasp my importance.

I wanted to feel like I belonged,
that I was part of something larger than myself.
Now I recognize I was—
I've learned that every person plays a role
in theater and in life.

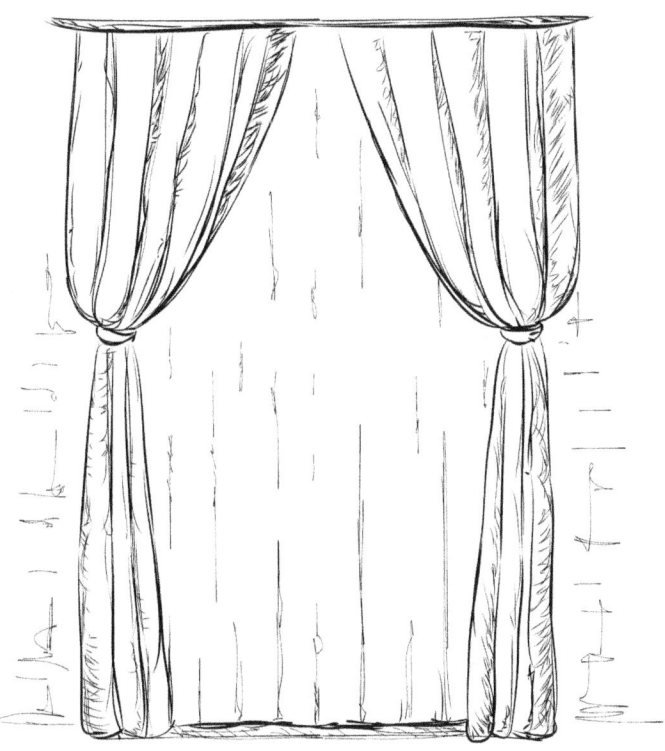

In the Air

In college, I signed up for Circus Skills
to fulfill my physical fitness requirement.
That same semester, I enrolled in Commedia dell'Arte
and Pantomime;
it was the semester I wanted to run away with the circus.

I learned how to stand on someone's head,
        how to walk on stilts,
        how to mime a box,
        how to play a mischievous-but-loving Arlecchina,
        how to make a mask out of paper mâché,
        how to juggle.

        But most importantly,
        I learned how to fly.

The silks seduced me;
I'd wrap myself in them,
cocooned in safety
above the ground
until I would
tumble down,
landing upon the mat.
Soaring high
despite the anxiety
that had
kept
my
two
feet
on
ground.

I saw myself within the tent,
holding onto the trapeze
as it
swang
left
        right
left,
took a leap of faith,
like the performers I had
seen
as
a
child
in
Cirque du Soleil.

I miss the time when
I dreamed of the circus
and could
have run away
to join one.

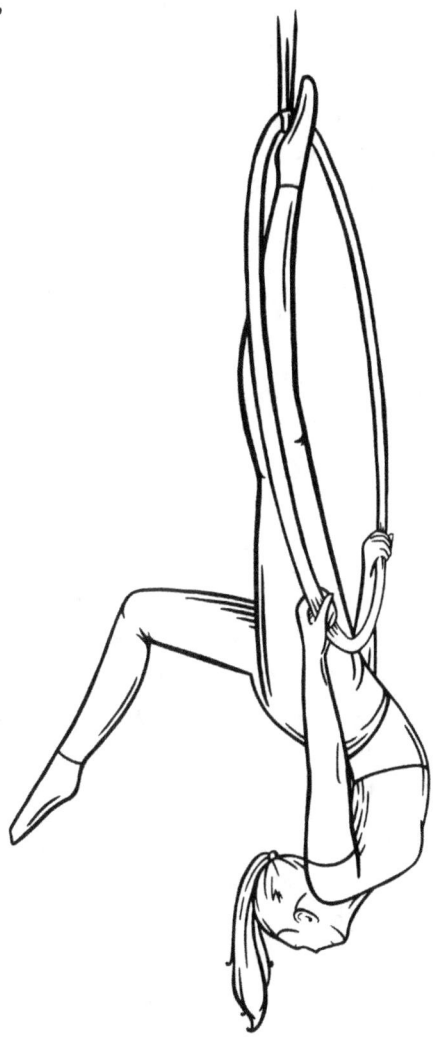

20/20 Vision

As a child, I loved to read and create stories in my head.
I sat on the floor at home, in the library, or in bookstores
at the mall
to devour books page by page.
Even before I could decipher the words on the page,
I would invent stories that matched the pictures.

In elementary school, we learned that my eyes were weak.
That they lacked the necessary
coordination; they were not team players.
They took more energy to operate;
they detoured my brain,
making reading nearly impossible sometimes.
I pushed through, wanting to escape
into the realm of make-believe,
even if my eyes didn't agree.

In fifth grade, my teacher wrote on my report card,
"Rebecca needs to read more at home."
But little did he know, I was devouring books—
it was hard for me to follow along in the classroom.
My eyes didn't want to play the same games as my peers;
they led me on their own adventures.

When I found the comment on my report card years later,
it stung. I thought this teacher saw me for who I was,
but I guess he was the one with the vision problems after all.

Spoiled Moments

I was a spoiled child,
and at times I believe I have grown
into a spoiled adult.

As a child, it was only
me, myself, and I,
and I often got
what I asked for
when I asked for it.

I traveled the world
and around my own city,
had adventures
at almost every turn.

I was lavished with presents
from family
as the youngest and only
girl in the room.

I got what I wanted
even when I didn't
deserve it—
a doll from Harrods
after the worst tantrum
I had ever had,
countless trips
to Disney World
where I slept in lavish hotels.

Now, as an adult,
I find it hard not to
treat myself to
theater outings, restaurants,
and lush surroundings.
I find it hard to say "no"
to events that
will drain my bank account,
to say "no"
to art.

Some days, I have to remind myself
I'm not a child in an adult body,
that I am more
than a girl holding a new doll,
insisting that it must be mine.

Pet Connection

When I was younger,
I wanted a pet.
My mom had a severe allergy to animals
of the cuddly variety,
so I had to do with fish, hermit crabs, and a lizard.
In those early days,
I watched the hermit crabs scuttle across the floor,
wishing I could hug them without fear of being pinched.

To fill the furry void left in my heart,
I spent time with my neighbors' cats:
Spunky, Kitty, and Clay.
They were sometimes friends,
sometimes frenemies,
sometimes just plain enemies,
but I loved them
and wanted them to love me back.
Clay loved eating French fries with ketchup from Roy Rogers;
Kitty was a princess, lusting after her desires;
Spunky was afraid of me at first but became my biggest fan.

After one vacation,
(probably to Newport, RI)
I came home to
no Clay,
no hermit crabs.

My grandmother had been pet-sitting my shelled critters,
Debbie and Cliff,
(you should never name pets after your parents),
and when it came time for them to change shells,
there was a disaster—
a mutiny that
ended with two casualties.
My poor grandmother had to share the bad news.

And my darling Clay had been sick for months,
and it was finally time to say goodbye.
I was told he walked proudly into the vet's office
on that last visit.
While I never got the chance to say goodbye,
I remember him often.

Do They Rescue Us, or Do We Rescue Them?

One summer,
a neighborhood cat,
Skinny,
took up residence underneath
the beach chairs in front of our house.
He loved Jewish deli and connection.
Where the other neighborhood cats were fearful and feral
and only came up to us because of our offered plates of crunchies,
Skinny was special.
He didn't want only the food
we gingerly provided.
He wanted affection.

One day he approached the door,
bloody and battered—
we will never truly know how.
He would become ours
through a series of random events.
He loved us and tolerated my overwhelming love for him.
It was poetic, I think, that he lived his youth on the streets
and spent his retirement in the warmth of a home
filled with love.
Although sometimes I think he stayed for the Jewish deli.

Nostalgic Viewpoint

I dip in and out of nostalgia
like a toe dips into a hot bath
or a cool dip into a pool
on a summer day.

I dip in and out of nostalgia
like sticking your hand out from
underneath your umbrella
to check for the light, passing rain.

I dip in and out of nostalgia
as the train lulls me like a lullaby.

My eyes heavy with sleep,
as trees and streams pass like an
abstract watercolor painting.

I dip in and out of nostalgia
until I wake with a start.

Outsiders

We were inseparable after school.

We were outsiders
who spoke fast and were wise beyond our years.
We learned about each other's faiths,
and our friendship grew outside of the confines
of the afterschool program.
First, we hung out with our parents in restaurants,
and soon, we'd be traveling the world by ourselves.

We were separated by distance
when you went off to college,
far from home,
but when you returned,
I got you a volunteer gig
on a political campaign;
we enjoyed a summer
of exploration in the city we loved
that's documented in the media
we consume.

Then, one day
we just
drifted apart.

I am not sure what you are up to these days,
but I hope you are well,
and finding joy and happiness
wherever you go.
You deserve it.

Pen Pals

Your hair was blonde,
as bright as the sun,
long, down past your waist.
You were new to the class and
could have been friends with anyone,
but you chose me,
the lonely first grader.

We talked so much,
moved around the classroom like
world travelers carrying
suitcases brimming with dreams,
dropping crayon shards
along the way.

Even changing schools could not keep us apart.
You transitioned from pal to pen pal;
our reunion in middle school
was bittersweet.

We were together
when the towers fell;
doves of peace perched
on your front lawn.
Then I watched you climb
the social ladder,
while I remained on
the bottom rung,
devastated.

We went off to separate high schools.
This separation different than the first—
I went to public school;
you went to private.
Being pen pals was no longer cool.

Our worlds collided for special celebrations,
and occasionally for the mundane,
like a trip to the movies.
Then—
true silence.

You became even more popular.
You pushed even harder.
You climbed to the top of success in your field.

Now we are on different ladders;
you climb yours, and I climb mine.
I wonder if you ever think of me,
if you ever remember
your first best friend.

Photograph of Memory

An astronaut and a dark fairy
smiling in a photograph,
ages fourteen and sixteen,
naïve to the world,
embracing the unknown
with teenage confidence.
A night of Halloween fun,
adventure.
All that remains
is the memory from
a now-gone photograph.

Then a tug of war
over an innocent heart,
a confused heart.
A deep cut of betrayal
against my chest.
More torn photographs.
Then rebirth and growth.
New love.
Chanced meetings and encounters brought
whirlwinds of pain, anger.
Building bridges requires permits
from both parties.
But the winds of change did not allow
smooth crossing.
Love was out
of the picture;
friendship, a sought-after dream.

The winds changed again,
turned the world
upside down,
ripped you away
when you were just a boy
finding out what it meant to be
a
man.

I can't bring myself to visit your grave.
How are we meant to grieve a person
we are supposed to hate?
The hate melted away years ago,
but feelings of loss remain.
We "didn't want"
to be friends,
but I was the one who was forced to accept that.
Now, only my side of the story remains—
we didn't understand the power we had
over ourselves, over each other.

I think of you often as you were
at sixteen, seventeen, eighteen,
a boy, not yet a man,
in the series of nostalgic memories,
how you smiled in that now-gone photograph
with my arms around you
from so many Halloweens ago.

Questions

You asked me what I thought about
as I drifted off to dreamland,
my fifteen-year-old brain unsure of why
you would want to know such a thing,
not realizing that each person
had a different routine,
saw different things
when heads hit pillows.
My reply through AOL was,
"I think of all of you.
I think of all the ways we can connect,
all the ways I can help,
all the things we would do."

I think this caught her off guard;
the words she sent in response
burned—
hurt the sweet, innocent girl
who wore her heart on her sleeve,
uncertain what to make of
her friend.

She and I would drift in and out of friendship;
I never really understood why.
Maybe that moment on AIM
was a warning
of what would come.

Perhaps I spent too much energy
trying to convince her,
change her.
Maybe I tried to save her one too many times
before I learned that it is nearly impossible to save
people—especially from themselves.

Celestial Conversations

I look up at the sky,
the sea of stars
obscured.
Raindrops beat against
the pane of glass.
A wandering mind
travels through time
and space,
observes the moon,
wonders about
the conversations
they may hold,
and grasps the silence.

Dreamland

I do not lie awake
in the darkness.

While you tell me about
how you toss and turn,
I speak the language of sleep.
My head hits the pillow,
and I drift off to a world
away from this one.

A world blended in possibilities and
impossibilities,
of memories,
of all that I have forgotten,
of all that I will remember
when I wake.

Gossip Chef

I love to dish out gossip,
but I often forget
that it can burn me
like a hot dish coming
off the stovetop.
I must wear gloves,
be careful,
alert.
I must remember,
to watch the pot
so nothing boils over.

Do You Remember?

I hold on to the blanket
I made for your darling baby girl
when she was born.
This year, she turns five.
Beyond the pandemic, our friendship
has been strained for some time.
I held out hope that I would return
into your life.
So I hold on to the blanket.

When we first met,
you wanted to beat me up—
you had me up against a wall,
saw that I was not a formidable opponent,
realized that perhaps I just didn't understand
the power of my own mouth.

I was protected by juniors and seniors,
but I don't think that is what stopped you
from hitting me in the hall that day.

Then I became your best friend.
I fought rumors with truth.
I fought for you.

I was there when you needed me.
I helped you succeed in your coursework,
told you to hold on during those cold and dark nights.
I helped you clean your house in preparation
for your father's arrival home.
You carved an "R" into your skin
to memorialize our friendship.

I held a piece of paper in my wallet for years
even though we had stopped speaking,
just in case.

You helped me form a wild streak,
or at least a mild one.
You took me places I had never gone before,
helped me experience more of what life had to offer.
We shared everything, raced
to each other's sides whenever we needed
a friend,
a protector,
an escape.
You held me when I grieved,
and
when I didn't know why
I grieved.
Until another friend took precedent.

She would be the one you would call at night.
The one who would be by your side.
The one you would fight with and for
and leave her clothes in a bag on her stoop.

I'm sure she knows your daughter,
but neither of you know
that I stare at the blanket
night after night
wondering if I will ever
pick up the phone.

Distance

The phone does not ring as much as it used to.
Stories that once flowed freely
now seem like distant memories
that flash and flicker over screens.
The silence of forgotten birthdays fills my feed.
We have grown apart
        only tied together
            by the strings of the path
                of the people I choose to follow.
I didn't even know that would be our last conversation.
If I knew,
        I would have hugged you tighter,
            laughed harder,
                taken that photograph,
but life builds voids that are impossible to fill.

Silence

Your absence speaks volumes.
The silence used to stab me in my chest;
my eyes used to well with acidic tears.
These days the silence is expected;
the pain has dulled.

I still wonder what happened to you
out in the great big world.
What joys and pain have filled your heart?
Do you remember me like I remember you?

You have turned into a ghost,
enveloped by smoke.

Will our friendship
ever be more than this?

They say time heals all wounds.
I can't say I agree.

One day, I will forget you
to make room for new friends,
to build a new me.

For now, I try to hold onto the
wisps of you
until I can set them free.

Sometimes

Sometimes,
we have to allow for flexibility
in our plans, our lives.
We have to follow our instincts
even if it means
our eyes well with tears.

Sometimes,
it means not knowing when
we will have the opportunity
to see a friend again.
We just have to trust
that our paths will cross.

Sometimes,
you know the right thing
is the hard thing.
The safer thing.

Sometimes,
you have to trust the universe
and the people in it.

Sometimes,
first meetings take
years to come to fruition.

Sometimes,
the internet fills the void.

Sometimes,
I imagine us meeting,
sharing photographs
during intermission at a Broadway show.

Sometimes,
I imagine us having drinks in a fancy hotel
surrounded by fancy people.
We talk and laugh for hours.

Sometimes,
I stare out the window on a rainy day,
knowing I made the right call—
but saddened that I had to do so.

Food Tour

late night drives
finding solace
in the arms of the dark sky

best friend in the driver's seat
I am in the passenger
streets familiar and foreign blur

dipping french fries into
hot fudge sundaes
then quesadillas
dripping cheese onto the dashboard
then milky and sweet coffee
cleaning the car
close to midnight
to leave no evidence
of this escapade

recovering from the storm
processing
graduation
roadmap missing
childhood washed away in the arms of the sea

retail job
knowledge
g
    a
        p
            s

learning how to be "professional"
intelligence often questioned
anxiety
tears
solidarity

back then
we had the freedom to do anything
but not the freedom to do everything

What We Lose

Superstorm Sandy stole my childhood,
turned my innocence into sea foam,
whipped through my home,
and sent a whirlwind through my life.

More than ten years later, I still feel like I am picking up the pieces,
              like I still am grieving,
                    filled with shame
                              and
                                        guilt
                    when the rest of the world has
                                        moved on
                                        forgotten.

One of the last physical reminders, a hat
that my parents grabbed for me;
it came in a blue NYC Marathon bag
              which I still have,
even though I was safe and warm in the arms of my boyfriend and his
family.

My community was
              dark
                        frigid
              damp
                        scared
essentially homeless
as the sea water
devoured our homes.

That October and November, I remember
being
dreadfully
cold.

One donation was a stack of hats and scarves,
everyone had them—
the same ones—
maybe they were supposed to be for the marathon runners,
the ones who couldn't run
in the dark.
It has ear flaps, a large poof;
I do not want to imagine a winter without it.
The thought of not having it feels like losing a piece of who I
was
on that night and the many
many
many
nights
that followed.
So I'll wear it as I pick up the pieces and
            grieve,
                    when the rest of the world has
                            moved on,
                            forgotten.

SELF-DISCOVERY

Mother Nature's Power

Leaves change
from green to red,
in a pattern only nature understands,
and humanity stares in awe.

Trees wave at me in the wind;
their leaves rain upon my head.
Other times, as the winds pick up,
I feel neither joy nor acknowledge their greeting.

Rain falls from the sky;
sadness and solace
alternate in every drop.
It is both a gift and a curse
of nature.

My stomach rises to my throat,
my brain sinks down into my soul,
my heart rattles in my empty chest.

I listen intently,
sorrow wrapped in the light,
joy lurking in the shadows.

I see Mother Nature in
the inevitable cycle of life and death.

Ocean Song

I have spent my entire life
by your edge.

I love the way your water
meets your sand,
the way the birds swoop
down to catch their prey,
the sounds they make in the process.
I love the smell of your brine,
the way your water tickles my toes.
I love being connected to something
so large.
I love floating,
watching the fish hurry past
from your edge.

In my saddest and my most joyful moments,
I run to you to celebrate or mourn.
It is there that I end up
sitting, staring into your abyss,
healing.

What We Carry

I have carried the weight of my past:
the pain and the joy,
trauma passed
generation
        to
           generation,
unresolved pain and hurt.
I'm learning that holding on
can be harder than letting go.
It's easier to speak.
I sit in therapy
or
listen to others
share their journeys of rebuilding,
transmuting their traumas
and anxieties to create something new,
something different,
something beautiful.
Then I remember I can do this too.
Slowly,
        day
           by
              day
I can loosen my grip on the past
and live in the
present.

Can Be

I can be
too afraid to speak up,
too afraid of being judged,
too worried about my oddities.

I can be
silent,
afraid to ask questions,
worried that the answers will terrify me.

The Storm

Your anxiety wells up like a storm.
Your ship, once even-keeled,
now jolts side to side.
What-ifs flash like lightning.
You are afraid to rely on your crew,
afraid you will terrify them,
afraid you will chase them off the ship,
even if it is the only way to prevent yourself from
d
r
o
w
n
i
n
g.

Lighting cracks
against the mast,
you must reach out—
if you don't, this catastrophe
will be your end.
You scream as loud as you can;
the wind howls
to match your intensity.

Once you break through,
the seas calm,
the clouds break,
the wind turns into a whisper,
and you turn to your crew,
and apologize for
scaring them.

The Great Lobby

I scream into the void,
stand in the lobby of this place
with its grand marble work and beauty,
and ask the world for answers
so I don't feel so aimless,
so lost.
So I can feel like I am on the right path,
certain that I am doing the right thing.

Bathtub

Anxiety, fear, and depression wash over me.
I step into the shower;
the water cannot wash away the things about myself
that I fear,
cannot stop the flood of my thoughts
as the basin overflows.
Stuck in this place.

My fear extends to this place;
maybe it's the birth of water that scares me,
maybe I learned about the horrors of humanity too young,
afraid of what a spout could bear—
gas.

I can fill a tub with my self-doubt.
Words, tumbling thoughts,
tumbling into the tub like
bubbles.

Pop, pop, pop.

Balloons float past my line of sight
A sweet sixteen of pinks, purples, blues,
silk flowers at every seat.
Cupcakes instead of cake,
the guy in a blue shirt
refusing to dance,
refusing to even consider the thought.
Someone talks sense for one photo,
one moment before I blow the candles into
darkness.

And I am back in the shower,
carrying basins back to the well.

This repetition of
to
fro
to
fro
carried through millennia.
We women carry,
congregate by the well
where the soul is borne from the earth.
We pull,
struggle in the heat of the sun,
gather to wash, clean, launder.

Launder what?
Clothes?
Walls?
Floors?
Souls?
Neshamah,
our life source,
the life source of the ones before,
weary of the spout.
I carry them into the tub too;
they are not here,
yet here they stand.
As one, as me.

Wounds
travel, dripping,
dribbling from the spout,
lost,
disaggregated from them onto me;
I am covered
in wounds and memories—
some that I have made,
others, the demons of anxiety—
yet others borne from the spouts of the generations
that came before,
that came *before the before* I even knew.
I know nothing of then,
just that I carry the wounds of my ancestors,
the words and wounds borne through the spout.

Acid Rebels

The acid in my stomach rebels.
This anxiety, ever-present.
While it doesn't define me,
it rotates around me,
a revolving door.
The exit is right there.
I move forward and backward,
and it's always
just out of reach.
I spin.

Am Yisrael Chai

Kol ode balevav p'nimah,
Nefesh Yehudi homiyah
In the Jewish heart,
A Jewish spirit still sings . . .

I stand alone, facing a sea
of photographed faces,
artifacts of the past,
belonging to the ones who came
before me.

Memories of Israel,
of Hebrew School,
of my Purchase senior project,
swell within my soul
as I try to remember these moments
gone by.

I am standing at Yad Vashem—
The Holocaust Museum—
on my Birthright trip,
confused about my connection to this place
and why I'm so far from home.

Walking into the gallery, I hear
small children learning
what it means to be Jewish.
I was their age when I first began to understand
my faith,
my religion,
my history.

When I first learned about
them.

They are singing
in the *shtetl*
in the home of my people
but not *my* home.

I remember the history I've been taught,
that before there was a State of Israel,
leaving the *shtetl* was a dream
afforded to only a small few.
I think about the journey my great-grandparents took
out of the east.
I think of my "cousin," Jean
with the numbers on her wrist,
and the stories she did not speak of.

Back to the children
singing on this recording:
Ulfa'atey mizrach kadimah
Ayin l'tzion tzofiyah
And the eyes look east
Toward Zion . . .

Did they know what they were yearning for?
They certainly had no idea what was to come.
They didn't know what would become of
their village,
their community.
their culture,
their religion,
their lives.

They didn't know their voices would be captured and replayed
in this museum for decades to come,
that people would cry when they heard
their sweet voices dreaming of a peaceful world.

Ode lo avdah tikvantenu
Hativkvah bat shnot alpayim
Our hope is not lost,
Our hope of two thousand years . . .

They were the voices of the children
yearning for a place
where it was not only safe but acceptable to be Jewish.
That place did not exist for this community.
They only knew antisemitism.
They only knew poverty.
They only knew their culture.
They maybe knew who they were:
Eretz Yiseral,
the people of Israel.

L'hiyot am chofshi b'artzenu
Eretz Tzion v'Yerushalayim
To be a free nation in our land,
In the land of Zion and Jerusalem . . .

Yet here I stand,
in one of the most contested places on Earth,
not sure of my identity,
but brought back to the present,
wrapped in the past.

Candle Glow

The glow of the candles
atop
a table strewn with unopened mail
frozen in time,
a pair of candlesticks
to remind us that we carry light,
to separate the week from the day of rest,
to show there is holiness and peace within and throughout.
We never really kept Shabbat—
or at least I never really kept Shabbat.
Those Friday nights of candle-lighting
were moments of reflection and connection
for those in the room and for those around the world
who were setting apart their weeks,
marking their weeks,
praying for peace, compassion, and kindness.
My neighbors
engulfed me in the world of pause.
We may still watch TV, turn on the stove,
load the dishwasher, read a book, or play a game—
activities that others would feel were prohibited
on this day of rest.
At the home across the way from ours,
lightly dressed as the heat poured in,
we carried our weeks with us,
each a different shape and weight,
recounting, sharing, relieving each other of the weight.
Maybe everyone was home.
Maybe only bits and pieces of the group would be there.
We would play and eat,
but I wonder if they stopped to see
the moment the candles glowed.

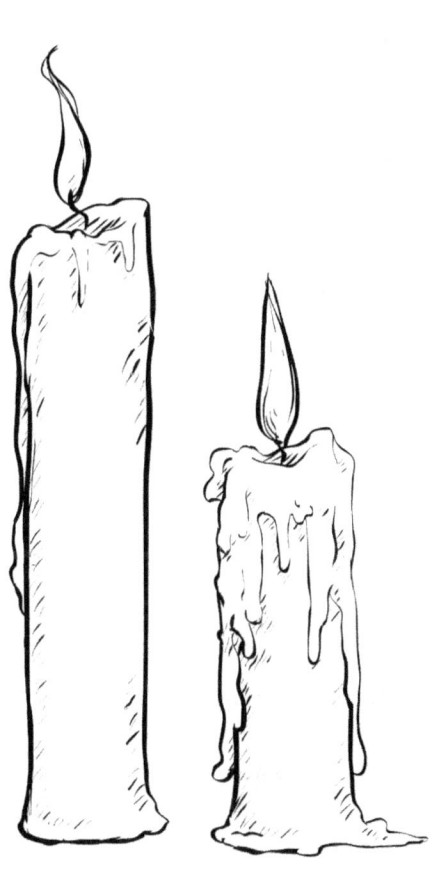

Jew "ish"

I can hear myself
singing loud and proud
from the front row
of my Hebrew school.
I can't remember which event
it was for, only that
I knew who I was,
what community I was a part of.

We sang joyful songs, prayer books in hand,
songs that reminded us
of who we are.

I knew I was Jewish from a young age—
I remember doing arts and crafts at holidays,
throwing sins into the sea,
eating apples dipped in honey,
matzo brie.
At all the appointed times of year,
I was told I was Jewish.

Shabbat candles with a TV blaring in the background,
my "big sisters" curled up on the couch,
laughing, giggling, playing games.
The phone would ring,
and it would be my parents,
telling me it was time to go home.
And through it all I knew I was Jewish.

In college,
I was president of Hillel.

I was the one who educated,
shared,
beckoned,
supported
what it meant to be Jewish on campus.

Then my trip to Israel,
instead of solidifying my faith,
confused me.
At some places I could feel
my ancestors' pleas
to be heard,
to be understood.
In others,
I heard the screams
asking how something like this
could be done.
Asking are we the
oppressed or the oppressor?

Walking around the world,
surrounded by the others,
I am
pork-eating,
hair-showing,
sometimes modest,
Torah-reading,
Mitzvah-doing,
not quite Jewish
but Jew "ish."

What-if Machine

I am a what-if machine—
I am free to admit that now.
I don't know when it started,
and I don't know if I ever had a life before it.
I remember learning to assess risk as a child,
determined to process every
situation and scenario that crossed my path.
Anxiety floods my pores.
I ask
what if
everything will be alright?

What then?

Darkness

Early morning, still dark.
Anxiety wells inside your stomach
flopping about like an
uncomfortable swarm of moths.
Anxiety doesn't have to win.
Breathe in.
Breathe out.
Close your eyes.
You are in control.

Morning Battles

The chilled breeze fills the room,
and all I want to do is remain wrapped in the warm cocoon
of your arms,
but the day calls us to move.

The sun is barely up; it is still dark.
My skin craves the touch of yours,
the warmth of the blankets.
I count to ten and prepare to don my wings—
but this pause becomes a cruel necessity to return to myself,
to remember the beauty hidden within.

I finally push through the cocoon.
Legs hang off the side of the bed
one step
then
another;
warmth subsides,
and
chilled tile
fills the void.
A shiver comes
as cold air
zooms past
a shower curtain.

My wings freeze.
I try to flutter the icy tendrils
o f f
in preparation for my
battle
as I turn the knob
of the iron giant,
and water comes
pouring down.

Drifting

Memories drift through the air like snowflakes.
Each thought, each moment, unique,
flying through time and space itself.
I place my anxiety on a flake
and watch it drift across my field of vision
until it is out of sight
and out of mind.

Parade Magic

Bubbles fill my line of sight.
Magic fills the air.
I smile.
You can see it in my eyes.
Joy exudes from my pores,
happiness only a parade can conjure.
Children wave wands, summoning more bubbles.
The main mouse stands and waves through the effervescent blur.
My stomach
flutters.
I am part of the magic;
the outside world melts away.
No emails, no drama, no anxiety.
I am in the moment, watching
my favorite characters dance along the route
as bubbles fill the air.

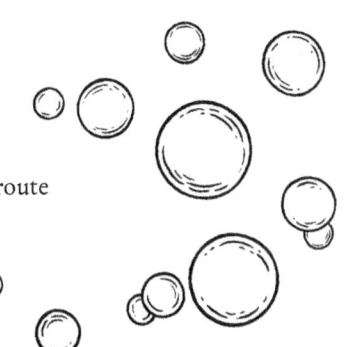

I Am Good

I say, "I am good,"
ready to tackle the new day.
But am I truly?
Or is that just a façade
I have built
around myself?

In therapy, I say,
"I am good,"
and then a jumble of words come tumbling out,
contradicting that statement.
Sure, I have daily improvement and
daily setbacks.
There is so much more to who I am and who I want to be than
a simple qualifier,
a simple response:
"I am good."

Alphabet Soup

I am like the alphabet:
    sometimes
        organized
        neat
        easy to sing;

    sometimes disorganized—

      a

       c a n

         o f

        a l p h a b e t

          s
           o
            u
             p.

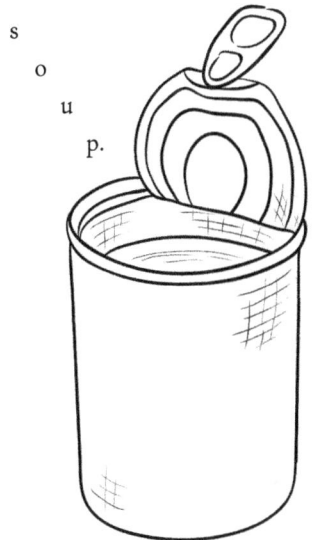

Interview Advice

They tell us, "Don't say 'problem-solver.'
Say 'solutions-oriented,'"
and loads of other crap when going out on interviews.
In one ear and out the other.
I am too human for many companies.
Marketing professionals urge their underlings to tell their stories,
live their most authentic lives—
yet, in interviews, I am told I am too unique.
That my attitude and resumé cannot be pigeon-holed into a single job.
That I wear too many hats.

I am left behind as others race ahead.
I am seen as a flight-risk
when all I want to do is find a place
where I can put down roots,
where I can truly be myself.

Chasing My Dreams

I lead others to their dreams
while still chasing my own.
Arms outstretched towards the
stars.
Skyscrapers tower around me.

I want to create,
    to sing off-key,
    to dance with no rhythm,
    to lose myself in the sounds of living,
    to discover the core
      of who I am
      and build a better version within.

Finding Self-worth

I am becoming comfortable with who I am
and who I want to be.
It has taken years to appreciate my weirdness, my eccentricities.

Bullies have attacked my self-worth before I could lock it away.
A small child who wore her heart on her sleeve,
who danced to her own rhythm,
who always lost her glasses and would lose
her head if it wasn't attached.
In spite of mean words and actions,
I am learning to love myself regardless of what anyone says.
I want you to know that it is okay to be who you are.

Qualifier

What is "good"?
      "bad"?
Why can't something just "be"?
Why can't I just "be"?
Why do I feel the need to
qualify
every action or reaction?

I am my own worst critic.
I can quell everyone else's imposter syndrome,
but when it is my own,
it is harder to pick away.

Then starts the spiral of self-hate and disdain.
No matter how much I just want to live and
not place judgments so harshly.
      Understand
            that moments can change and adapt
            that growth looks different for everyone
            that you can learn to support yourself
                  as well as you support others.

Perfect Size

You know you are the perfect size.
You know to love your body for what it provides
and how it allows you to participate in the world,
but sometimes society gets into your head,
says you are too small or too big.
The worst is when you put on a dress you love,
a dress you trust to make you feel like a princess.
You stare at the dress;
you know there is a chance it may not fit.
It is old,
but it was your go-to for special occasions.
You rush around the house getting ready to go out.
You grab the dress out of the closet, and now it won't zip.
You have a million backups—you are one of the lucky ones—
but at that moment, none of them compare.
Your back is too wide; you don't even know when that happened.
You are left standing in front of your bathroom mirror in tears.
You run out the door in a backup dress others love, but your mind is
on the dress left in the bag that you can't wear.

Shouldn't Matter

It shouldn't matter what I wear—
I should be able to wear whatever makes me happy.
I shouldn't have to worry about what some dude will say about me as I
cross the street
       as I wait for a Lyft
       as I study in a classroom
       as I sit in the library
       as I shop in a store
       as I sit in a theater.
We should celebrate our bodies and express ourselves
in the ways that brings us joy.
It shouldn't matter what we wear—
women should be able to wear what makes us happy.

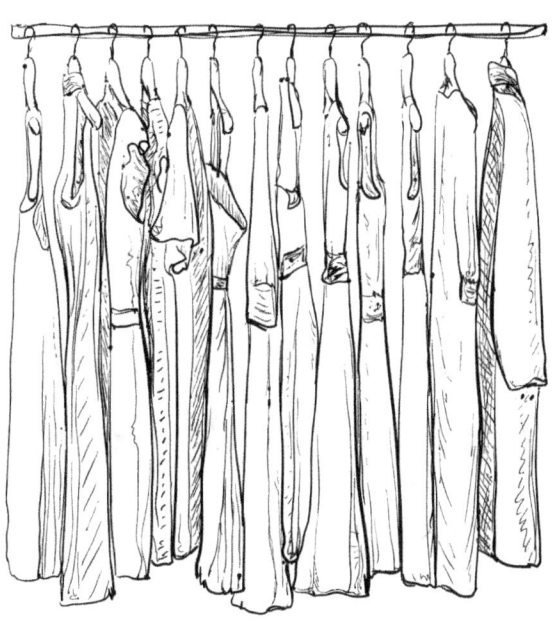

Superstition

Brown
  morning coffee
  a piece of cake
  the color of my grandmother's superstition.

When seeking the perfect gift
she would ask
  red or
  beige or
  brown?
  (The last signaling doom.)

Trauma breeds superstition—
or is it the reverse?

Familial Navigation

Family can be difficult
        to navigate
        to understand.

Whether it is the family we received by blood,
gifted at birth,
or the ones we choose,
we are forced
        to learn to read people
            situations
        to become an individual
            apart from the whole.

For some, it is easy;
For others, it is impossible.

Material Transcendence

When I was young,
my grandma asked
what I would like from her
apartment before she died.

I hated the question.
I didn't want to think about
taking things away from her,
away from her home.
It didn't feel right,
but she kept asking
what I wanted from the home she made
from almost nothing.

I took the Hubbell figurines,
the *Lord of the Rings* ones,
her beloved rocking chair,
and a few other odds and ends.

I stare at the rocking chair now
and envision her there,
sewing,
watching TV,
smoking a cigarette.
Sometimes being this close to the things she loved
makes me miss her more,
but most of the time I am happy that
I have her with me every day.
That my life is infused with her
and with the belongings
she loved.

Passing

I was there the moment she passed.
I was one of her many loved ones in the room.
I sang to her my favorite Hebrew prayers,
whispered in her ear.
I was there as her eyes darted across the room
             as she took her last breath.

Even though we knew
we didn't have many moments left,
maybe a few hours or a few days,
her final moment was heartbreaking.
I dropped,
fell through the floor.
No one really can teach you how to say goodbye
until you are in the moment
or until the moment passes,
and there is no goodbye.

Sense Them with Me

They may be gone,
yet I still sense them with me.

I can

      hear them say my name,
      hear them greet me in the hallway,
      smell their apartments,
      feel their kisses across my cheek.

I remember

      the way we made monster mash with what you had in cupboards,
      sitting by the pool's edge playing Scrabble and trips to the library,
      the time I hid under the table so well you thought I was missing,
      the moment we shared before I would enter the elevator as I said,
      "see you later, alligator."

I can

      see your bright purple eyeshadow as my mom tries to
      blend it away,
      smell the coffee brewing, cigarettes you haven't
      smoked in decades,
      hear the muffled TV from your bedroom,
      feel the cream-colored shag carpet against my toes,
      see your long skirts drift across the floor at the mall
      as I scream, "NO MORE DIAMONDS!"

I can

      feel them around me
        always,
          forever,
            living on in my heart.

Yizkor

Grief can be a funny thing—
you think you can be done grieving,
then, all of a sudden, your pain
reintroduces itself.
The heartache and tears reemerge.
I push the feelings down,
ashamed,
wondering if I am alone in this grief that
I was told should have passed.

Yet year after year, my faith encourages me
to remember the ones I have loved and lost,
ones that have returned to the earth,
to their Creator,
their memory, a blessing.
And there I am, prayer book in hand,
heart pounding,
hands shaking,
tears pouring,
no tissue in sight as I think to myself,
I can't believe I am crying again.
Everyone around me seems to hold their grief within, but
I want to shout mine from the rooftops.

The prayer concludes.
The moment passes.
Or does it
embed itself into the fabric of my soul
where a scent on the wings of the wind
sends me back to you?

Hugs

I carry
warm hugs
in my pocket
like a ring of keys.
It is so much more than
the simple act of holding:
it is the guarantee of safety,
of your love.

It reminds me I am
human—
that we are connected
no
matter what.

When anxiety wells,
when fear bounds,
when tears drip down my chin,
when I feel alone,
I dip into my reserve of your hugs
deep within my soul;
I gently search
that deepest pocket,
afraid I may run out.
I tap into them when
I need you near me.

COMMUNITY & ME

Powerline of Art

From the train,
I can
see
graffiti lining the walls of the city.
Bright colors,
lines, and shapes—
images filled with talent
tagged against bland walls
faded with time.
The history of a city
provides the walls with
character.
It speaks of adventure, community, rivalry.
Stories of communities
finding voices in the darkness,
standing up against the status quo.

Love, Love, Love

Grand Central Station
in New York City
is a special place
for my husband and me.
In our early years of dating,
when I was still young,
naïve to the world,
deeply in love—
and in love with the idea of being in love—
we would meet in the lower level on a bench
across from Junior's.
That was our place.
As I would get off the Times Square Shuttle,
my stomach would flop, and my heart would flutter.
I would run down to that lower level
and into the arms of my love.
Excited to see the city through a new pair of eyes.
Excited to be warm and cozy in the arms of my love no matter the
weather.
Excited for whatever the day's journey had in store for us.
Excited at the possibilities of what life had in store for us.
Ready to set out into our lives
right out the doors of Grand Central Station.

Grand Central Station

the tunnel into
grand central station
dark dotted with light
at the end of the tunnel
grandeur—
the great meeting hall
people rushing along
beauty escaping them
then those with their heads staring up into
the only sky where city dwellers can see the stars
then me stopping to marvel at this moment

Train Windows

I have pressed my face against the glass
of every train window
I have ever met.
I know it is
                 unsanitary
                 unnecessary
but I love watching the world zoom by,
seeing the world through landmarks—
places I have never been and may never go.
When I turn away from the world,
my eyes dart around the car;
people enter and exit, each of our stories separate
but intertwining as the train speeds on.

Street Music

A traffic light

red
yellow
green

helping to determine order.

One car passes, then the next,
then an old woman with her shopping cart,
more cars.

Day in and day out,
the traffic lights create
the music of the streets.

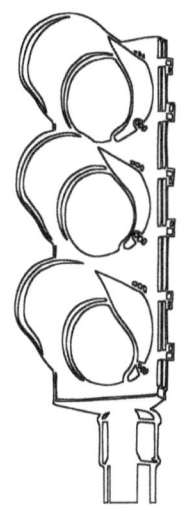

Metal Zooming

From the train window,
the world blurs.
Many trees become one,
cars race on the highway,
storefronts zoom past.
People on platforms waiting to board
stand behind the yellow line.
A myriad of parking lots appears,
people putting on the green,
completely unaware of the
force of metal zooming by.

Mortality

A hospital comes into view
along the train tracks.

Within its walls,
people celebrate and mourn
three hundred-and-sixty-five days a year.

No vacation
from sickness,
from mortality.

Stand Together

The city is dark.
Fog encroaches,
settles block by block,
a scourge that
may just
destroy us.

One by one,
we are forced to run.
Safety
eludes us time and again.
We must find the friend amongst the foes,
must stand together
to endure
the fall.

Medical Mayhem

I have
sat in pain,
whimpering alone,
a mound of anxiety,
wondering if the pain was my fear.

I made excuses for not going to the doctor,
pretended I knew what I was doing,
that I was fine even though I could barely
drag myself out of bed,
paranoid that I did this to myself.
That somehow I was making it all worse.

Coughing in fits,
unable to breathe,
my joints ached,
my eyes too afraid to see what was in front of them,
but more than willing to look into the depths beyond.

The world was muted;
my depression and anxiety controlled my every move
until the day I made the choice to try.

First the eye doctor,
but they were closed,
so I chose to address the cough.
A kind doctor met me,
and his Jewish humor comforted me.
For the first time in a long time,
I wasn't afraid to talk about
the welts practicing their disappearing act on my torso,
my nose clogging to the point of pain,
my stomach hurting and not at the same time.

I had practiced revealing these medical woes to friends,
family,
coworkers,
but never to a professional,
too afraid they would tell me it's just in my head.

But he listened and
gave suggestions,
assured me that what I was going through was real,
no matter how much I doubted it.

Acceptance

Everything changed in an instant;
the world came to a grinding halt, became quiet.
Sidewalks and roads lost their hustle and bustle.
It became harder to be present in the moment
and to be surrounded by those who you love the most.

The gears within my brain intensified,
sent an overload of signals—
the rushing train
that passed every empty station.

I was afraid to step foot
outside my door
until
the sun dawned
on my 30th birthday.

This birthday was supposed to be a landmark,
one to remember forever:
a trip to the Caribbean with my mom.
Ocean views, massages, luxury.

It became a birthday I would never forget—
on my lawn.
My parents and closest friends "surprising" me
with a car parade, blasting showtunes, pizza, and a piñata.
Then the winds changed.

My dad became sick.
They said he didn't have COVID,
but how could it be his heart?

As the mayhem subsided,
as he recovered,
I learned that everything could change in an instant.

On my birthday, I felt joy for the first time in weeks.

COVID Trails

Each morning,
I think about the way COVID steals away
senses,
people,
lives,
leaving a trail of brain fog
in its midst.
To avoid
the building anxiety,
I bring my hand to my nose
to smell the scent
my hand soap leaves behind,
taste the refreshing mint of my toothpaste.
COVID has rampaged too long in this city;
my body already houses fatigue, coughs, and joint pain.
The virus had to pick symptoms
I already have.
Why couldn't it give us blue spots or turn our ears green—
a visible mark that you are afflicted
instead of being masked
behind
a
cough
or a
sneeze?

Apartment

My apartment is tiny:
the size of a postage stamp
with a bathroom, kitchen, bedroom, living room,
and three large closets.
It is small, but it is ours.
It isn't perfect, but it sheltered us
while the world disintegrated around us.
I try to appreciate, find beauty even
in its cheap, white paint,
thin cream-colored carpeting,
figures and books lining the walls,
the piles of clothes,
and random memories scattered almost everywhere.
I have the privilege of love, safety, and warmth.
Maybe, just maybe, I can learn to love this physical space.

Lullaby of Sounds

There is a me on
the bus of memory
that is staring at the sky,
which is a cityscape.
Bright lights
even though it is night.
They sing softly to me,
as if a lullaby.
A sweet melody of car horns,
other wordless melodies.
I know this city is forever home.
The silence is jarring
when home used to be a hodgepodge of sounds.
It's too quiet in this new neighborhood, and this
version of me, within my brain,
hates the silence.
She creates her own version of street nose
in the hopes she
can fall asleep to bright lights and bright sounds.

COVID Capture

Sleep has eluded me in the last few weeks.
First the hours cut short, running from
adventure to adventure,
place to place,
meal to meal,
person to person,
trying to cram as much activity and life as possible in
      a day
      a week
      a year.

Then came the exhaustion.
At first it was a solid one,
one only felt when life was lived to the fullest.
I was out before my head would even hit the pillow.
But then it grew malicious—
a virus that weaseled past my defenses,
invaded my space.

I knew something was wrong as the plane descended
into the airport.
Something didn't feel right.
I've flown my entire life,
but my eyes and brain felt explosive.
Sleeping in my own bed didn't defuse the feeling.
I opened an inbox filled to the brim—
152 emails I had missed
trying to escape
to a warmer climate.

Then came the time to take the test that gripped the nation.
For the first time in practically three years,
the line appeared.

The virus
found a host in me.
Nestled in my trusty love seat,
tossed and turned for days on end,
never comfortable.
Emotionally,
physically
drained.
Watching *The Simpsons*
then *Criminal Minds* in an attempt to give
my brain some stimulation and relief.

I refused to take a sick day,
afraid of the judgment,
blamed myself for getting sick.
I pushed and I pushed,
trying to be my best self
in the face of this invisible monster.
I pushed and I pushed
to stare at the computer,
pretend that I was okay
when I was anything but.
When I was afraid to close my eyes,
scared I'd forget how to breathe during the night.

Then finally,
I took the time I needed to rest and recuperate.
Mentally preparing myself for the time
the cycle would begin again
when my husband comes home sick.

Broken System

I can't believe we live in a country,
in a world, where
medical treatment is not guaranteed.
I have had the privilege of healthcare for most of my life.
      I never
            had to wonder what would happen in an
                  emergency
            had to self-treat because I could not afford
                  treatment
            had to wait more than a few days for acute
                  and preventative care.

I have watched doctors save lives,
but today I stand at a crossroad,
staring at numbers and words on my screen.
I am not only out of my element but out of my league.
I wonder where my care will come from
when the price exceeds what I make in a year.
How I could end up in a debt so high
that I could never reach the top floor—
that this is a reality for countless people
in this country alone.
Yet we don't look for long-term solutions,
only quick fixes.
But I'll sit in this pain for all of us,
fearing that one slip
                  could change everything.

Realism vs. Magic

As a child,
I saw the world
as a mystical place
      where shadows are mischievous
      where genies live in lamps
      where carpets fly
      where mermaids swim
      where animals speak
      where trees talk
      where drawings on urns come to life.
I saw a world of problems with magical solutions.

As an adult,
I still see the world
as a mystical place,
but now I can see
      the pain of men stealing our rights
      the suffering of those escaping abuse and war
      the hunger that fills the halls of our schools
      the thirst for knowledge stolen from the cup
      the deforestation that silences the animals
      the droughts that prevent earth from growing
      the pollution that fills our lungs until we can't

B
R
E
A
T
H
E

I have lived through global disasters,
have tried to understand them to no avail.
And I yearn for the magical solutions of my childhood.

Run to the Stage

I wonder if it would be fun to reinvent myself,
create a new me for the world to see,
take on a character that I have never experienced before,
run away for a brief moment
from the person I am
to a world where a better version of me exists.
I'd relish in the beauty of their world
while hiding from mine.

The After

After tragedy,
we say such and such place
is strong,
that the people and community are strong—
which they are,
but they shouldn't have to be.
They shouldn't have to feel the pain of loss
in a public forum.
The news vans will zoom in the days and weeks to come
until tragedy breaks somewhere else.
Then, the vans leave,
shifting the world's attention to the next
neighborhood,
village,
town,
city,
that is facing
unsurmountable
pain,
and you are left sitting in the wake,
trying to sort out your feelings.
You may even experience people saying that what you lived through is a
hoax.
Why do we continue to let this happen?
In homes, schools, movie theaters, places of worship, malls,
and so many other places where people gather.
We can do better in this country
to protect the people
of this country.

Running on Empty

I am running on a type of empty—
that
      a cup of coffee
         or
      a new tank of gas
                 can't truly fill.
A feeling so deep yet so shallow.

The proverbial glass
is only ever half-full or -empty.
How do you see the world?

What makes you feel full?
                Empty?

I don't know what to do with the sinking feeling;
the blood is running from my veins into
some unseen place
halfway across the world.

I lay my head down every night; my eyes slam shut,
not even long enough to say good night, and then I wake up,
hopeful that the world may just be a small iota better—
but I don't know if that is even possible.

I don't know if I am depressed
or anxious,
but I am in a place of desperation,
a whirlwind of uncertainty.

Often I am afraid to disclose pieces of me.
I am an open book, but I feel
                    guilt for my honesty
                    guilt for feeling
                    guilt for anger and for frustration.

Still, my words flow with few filters.
Yet, there is always some expression that is blocked,
                    that my fingers won't hit the keys
                    that my eyes won't see
                    that my ears won't hear
                    that my mouth won't speak
                    that my heart won't feel.

I am running on empty.

Twins

Doubt and failure live hand-in-hand:
I see them daily.
Some days, I evade these debilitating twins;
on others, I am lost in the whirlwind.

Clichés

We are told to run away from clichés,
but I am often wrapped in their comfort,
in their familiarity.

Should Be

I should be

           sleeping
           catching up
           running to catch a train
           anything but frozen
           caught between reality
           and my own personal hell

Analysis Paralysis

Still
frozen,
trapped in the process,
unable to choose.
I am a victim
of analysis paralysis.
But am I a victim
if my paralysis is caused
by an unending joy?
I walk through
city blocks
filled with
the new
married
to the old
and
smile,
frozen,
trapped
in
understanding
that you can do
countless things
in one
life.

Belief

I believe
       in the universe
       in faith
       in hope
       in hard work
       that we are all connected
       that we all have gifts
       in the power of choice
       in my heart
       all we have to do is be open

Hearts

Why are we so judgmental
When we can only name our own feelings?
When we cannot name someone else's pain?
Where we see the world through only our own eyes?

Can I trade my heart for yours?
Perhaps for a day
or
l   o   n   g   e   r?
I want to feel your pain and joy.
Erase my judgment,
so I can empathize with your beating heart.

Learning to Grow

When you grow a garden,
you have to think of so many things.
Yet you are returned to nature
with your hands in the dirt.
You grow roots in the garden
just like the flora you plant.
You weed the space,
you water it when needed,
you go there just to sit and be present in nature.
After you infuse love into your garden.
The fruits of your labor begin to peek through—
tomatoes, zucchini, peppers of all shapes and sizes.
You are nourished now, physically,
by the work of your garden.
Then it is time to say goodbye for the season.
You will be left with the memories, the recipes,
the photographs,
and the memory of the feeling your hands first felt
in the mud.

Garden of Life

Each flower in the gardens that we plant
has roots and a stem
through which nutrients are shuttled
to all areas of its being.
It helps create beautiful flowers
that make our eyes marvel at their splendor.
It then helps turn those beautiful flowers
into buds for vegetables
that will provide sustenance
to us and to the world.
Each stem, leaf, bud, and root
is important to its creation.
Each has a role it must play
just as we each have a role we play
to bring beauty, joy, and sustenance into
the world.

ACKNOWLEDGMENTS

To my parents: Debra Cavan and Cliff Bruckenstein, who have cheered me on and supported me my entire life and provided countless opportunities for growth and discovery.

To my husband, John Falzerano, thank you for standing next to me and holding me through all the different seasons. I am grateful that I met you at a Sweet Sixteen many years ago and that we continue to have adventures together. To many more wonderful years filled with adventures and love.

To my extended family: Uncle Ira Peterman and Eric DeLeon, Aunt Alice Bruckenstein and Steve Greenfield, Dawn and Larry Baker, Mark and Rhonda Kramer, Wayne Baker and Jessy Cronin, Chris Jannessen, Allison and Ryan Nichol, Nancy Moonves, Christine Falzerano, Peter Falzerano and Josette Mancini, Steven Falzerano, Anne Bradford, Mike Bradford, and Bobby Bradford.

To the people I carry in my heart: Grandpa Jerry Bruckenstein, Great-grandma Ethel (Mama) Muthig, Uncle Kenny Kramer, Alma Gold, Uncle Harold Cavan, Great-uncle Harold Peterman, and Jacob Vogelman.

To my home across the way: Francine Canin, Anna Genoese, Lisa and Matt Fekett, Christina Genoese, and Richard Canin and Jackie Burris.

To Morgana Watson, Alex Palmatier, and Jennifer Carroll for reading through all 200 of my poems to help me select the ones included in this collection.

To Michelle Hessing and Stephanie Blum, for being amazing friends who are always there for me.

To my stellar writing group crew, Alex, David, Monica, Koura, and Spacey, led by the amazing Nora Raleigh Baskin with whom I have been writing many days throughout the pandemic and beyond.

To the Showhoppers—you know who you are—thank you for being an amazing group of friends who I love to spend time with.

To my colleagues at the University of Bridgeport for their professional guidance and for the amazing support that has been provided to me, including the team in the Office of Student Academic Success who has been there in good times and rough times.

To my incredible teachers who have led me to have the skills to put this collection together, including the beloved Kay Capo.

To the amazing staff at Pure Ink Press for helping me bring this book to life; Leila Summers for her amazing knowledge and endless support, John Chancey for his marketing guidance, Kristin Gustafson for helping to create and grow the soul of this book. Miko Marsh and Elina Oliferovskiy for helping make this book stronger.

To the Patrons Circle at Seed&Spark for the generous donation to make my campaign a success and to Seed&Spark for all their support during the campaign phase of this project.

And to my kitty-cat family, Mr. Skinny, Sunshine, Henry, Twilight, Clay, Spunky, Kitty, Queenie, and Willow.

And to those who supported my book campaign at the Poet in your Pocket perk or higher:

Alice & Steve, Alisa, Anne, Ariel, Bartholomew, Bill, Brittany, Bryan & Lori, Claudia, Claire & Marc, Christine, Dave, David, Dawn & Larry, Debra & Cliff, Elena, Emily, Esther & John, Francine, Holly, Ilene & Harvey, Jamie, Jennifer, Jinny, Joanna, John D., John F., Julie, Karen & Neil, Laura G., Laura S., Leslie, Lillian, Luisa, Matthew, Melissa & Navid, Meredith, Morgan, Morgana, Moshe, Myia, Neil, Nurjahan, Paula, Payton, Peter & Josette, Robert, Sandra, Shelby & Mike, Simone, Stephanie B., Stephanie M., Stephanie P., Steven, Susan P., Susan S., Tim, Tobi & Denny, Valeria, Virginia, Yvrose.

To absolutely everyone who has in some way contributed to making this moment a success. THANK YOU!

www.ingramcontent.com/pod-product-compliance
Lightning Source LLC
Chambersburg PA
CBHW070717130626
46552CB00005B/2038